I0813140

PETS IN THE WILD!

HAMSTERS IN THE WILD!

Cody Koala

An Imprint of Pop!
popbooksonline.com

Hello! My name is Cody Koala

This book is filled with videos, puzzles, games, and more! Scan the QR codes* while you read, or visit the website below to make this book pop.

popbooksonline.com/hamster

*Scanning QR codes requires a web-enabled smart device with a QR code reader app and a camera.

abdobooks.com

Published by Pop!, a division of ABDO, PO Box 398166, Minneapolis, Minnesota 55439.

Printed in the United States of America, North Mankato, Minnesota.

052024
092024

Cover Photo: Shutterstock Images
Interior Photos: Shutterstock Images, Getty Images
Editor: Elizabeth Andrews
Series Designer: Laura Graphenteen; Neil Klinepier

Library of Congress Control Number: 2023947467

Publisher's Cataloging-in-Publication Data

Names: Hansen, Grace, author.
Title: Hamsters in the wild! / by Grace Hansen
Description: Minneapolis, Minnesota : Pop!, 2025 | Series: Pets in the wild! | Includes online resources and index
Identifiers: ISBN 9781098246143 (lib. bdg.) | ISBN 9781098246709 (ebook)
Subjects: LCSH: Hamsters--Juvenile literature. | Wild animals--Juvenile literature. | Wild animals as pets--Juvenile literature. | Rodents--Juvenile literature. | Rodents--Behavior--Juvenile literature.
Classification: DDC 636.0887--dc23

Table of Contents

Chapter 1

Hamsters

Hamsters are **rodents**. The German verb *hamstern* means "to hoard." Hamsters earned this name for their habit of storing lots of food in their cheek pockets.

Watch a video here!

Hamsters are **omnivores**. In the wild, their diet is mainly made up of seeds, grasses, and insects. Their teeth help them nibble, grind, and chew food.

Hamster **species** in the Middle East have been known to hunt in groups to find insects.

Chapter 2

Wild Hamsters

Hamsters are native to much of Europe and Asia in countries such as Greece, Syria, Belgium, and northern China. They live in areas that are warm and dry such as deserts.

Where Some Wild Hamsters Live

Asia

Belgium

Europe

Syria

Greece

China

Africa

N

W

E

S

Learn more here!

Hamsters are very good diggers!

Hamsters are nocturnal. In the daytime, they stay in their underground **burrows**. They come out at night to find and hunt for food.

Most hamster **species**, such as the Syrian hamster, are solitary. This means they live alone. They are also **territorial**. Some hamster species are social. Dwarf hamsters are often found in pairs in the wild.

dwarf hamsters

Chapter 3

Pet Hamsters

Syrian hamsters are the most popular pet hamster **species**. In 1930, scientist Israel Aharoni discovered a mother Syrian hamster and her young in the wild. Soon, hamsters were popular pets.

There are around 20 species of hamsters. Just five are common as pets.

Chapter 4

Caring for Hamsters

Hamsters are relatively easy pets to care for. They do not need walks, grooming, or too much interaction. However, they do need a safe, clean space to live with fresh food and water.

Some pet hamsters are OK with being held if it is done safely and properly.

A hamster's **enclosure** should be roomy with a secure lid. It should have bedding that is deep enough for the hamster to **burrow** in. Hamsters need places to hide, things to climb up, and toys to chew on. They love exercise wheels!

Pellet food is available for hamsters. Hamsters can also be fed small amounts of greens and certain vegetables and fruits. Food should always be placed in a clean dish. Fresh water should be given through a sipper tube.

Making Connections

Text-to-Self

What do you like best about hamsters?

Text-to-Text

Have you read any other books about hamsters? What did you learn in those books that was not in this one?

Text-to-World

There are many types of rodents people keep as pets, including guinea pigs, rats, and gerbils. What kind of rodent would you like to have as a pet?

Glossary

burrow – a hole that an animal digs in the ground for shelter; to dig.

enclosure – a type of secure container meant to keep a pet animal safe.

omnivore – an animal that eats both plants and other animals.

pellet – a small rounded piece of food.

rodent – any of several related animals that have large front teeth for chewing, including mice, squirrels, and beavers.

species – animals that look alike and can have young together.

territorial – characterized by the need to protect one's home.

Index

Online Resources

popbooksonline.com

Thanks for reading this Cody Koala book!

This book is filled with videos, puzzles, games, and more! Scan the QR codes* while you read, or visit the website below to make this book pop.

popbooksonline.com/hamster

*Scanning QR codes requires a web-enabled smart device with a QR code reader app and a camera.